# Ego Ignoscor

Lola

# Ego Ignoscor

A Collection of Poems

By Lola

# Lola

For my Mother, Father,

Sister, Brother, and Nicole.

# Lola

# BOOK ONE

Lola

1

The fingers touch the water.

Cool the earth into dying time.

Whisper my heart into the love of your ear.

With fear none it calls upon you,

A sound of the garden rose.

Tip-toes the solemn moment,

On the ground of earth's rare feet.

Do you trust me that I am yours,

And shall only lift you to greater floors,

To behold the sky of shaken glass,

Through which all the world you will see?


Be with me

In one graceful stare.

We shall rise above our death-made bones.

You wait so fast to call my name,

But these dimensions are hidden from your common ear.

I call from within you and your living soul—

Only that you will wait to hear these words divine.

Oh that you melt in madness of once believing,

And lend to me your eyes perceiving.

The messages travel in spiral waves,

With songs of saints and lonesome graves.

The silence paves a road to the sun,

And of this place I walked alone.


Come into being and I will hold you near.

We are like children alone in the world.

We are mad with passion,

And foolish as much.

May you feel the tender touch.


There is water in the sky

That rains upon you.

May you know that I am real.

Earth, Mercury, Jupiter, Uranus, Mars,

Neptune, Venus, Saturn, the infinite stars,

The beginning of all that never began,

Crying for love the outstretched hand,

And I was with you when we fell into this life,

And I am with you still.


We are pure and perfect together.

Our dreams are like candles that burn in our hearts.

It becomes with freshness to become a flower.

It is the night sky that makes us wait.

Give me your love and wait for me,

As for you I wait eternally.

2

There became a sacred wind

That through my head moved.

With wild mushrooms and golden skies

It walks in the morning of overwhelming scent.

It pushes the moon to its resting place,

Far from fettered fictions and opacities oblong.


So simply it spoke when I listened there

Of endless generations walking in line

And a heart that will always beat.

And with the soul we do breathe

Out volcanoes of upward stares.

And the walk the upside-down becomes,

Inside-out is strange to see.


Then I to rest on rocks and rivers,

Where it was brought to place,

As on both sides became the symmetry

Of this human face.

If only my hand was lighter ere then,

Then you would have known

To trust no more my confused words,

For truth they had not shown.

But then today began the day,

I swear to you it's true,

That I was all alone,

And only thought of you.

But you you were many

Of what I once had seen,

And all of us were living

In a living dream.

It was not I that placed the stars

So far for you to see,

But if you must then come along,

And there we shall truly be.

## 3

Rest now in the arms of open day—

Open like the stillness of a new bride's smile

That walks the isle of first love.

Hold the hand of the infinite child—

For he is your creation.


Will you trust the mindless game?

It is of thought you cannot believe.

Will you trust?

And if you trust,

Will you believe?


A saltwater sea has rushed my bones.

The forest has grown from the rootless tree.

I had no hope but to pray,

And this be the sea.


The corner of the room was the world,

So my arms fell towards the ground

As I lifted towards the sky.

I pinned my heart to the wall,

Then drew a picture of my dreams.

And nothing's what it seems.

And the day's love gleans.


I wait for God's voice as I wait for redemption.

I will admit my shame.

And all that I know I am lost the same.

And I know not how we came to be,

Nor why it is the beauty we see,

And though it be I live with pain,

I long never to leave this place—

Or will death show God's face—

Or have I seen?

4

Aloof atop the fragmented filament

That burns with billows of burning love,

Lightness has leaped into the stranger,

And I am now his only way.


Upon the segment that severs the seasons,

Alone with the ghost that severs the sky,

So it was to the wilderness was welcomed

The ancient hands of graceful time.


And the hands touch the mind and always

Will they leave us better then.

It was here we walked with fathomless feet

And let not the eyes grow old and stale!


The burning chimney cloaks the room,

Filled with rage, and pain, and doom.

Watch his feet, they cannot cease,

For as they roam, they find no peace.

And the house is inside the heart,

And the heart is inside the man.


Reach and reach, then reach no more,

Other worlds you cannot take.

Why it is you shiver?

Why it is you shake?


Your soul it runs before you,

And true it does adore you,

So why have you feared

The destruction of five senses?


See in the flesh the garden and the river:

The silence is servant,

The sun is shining,

And entwined divinely is the mystery lining.

Grant me this wish, for I am yours,

Or such it is the heart implores.


Beat the bristle and tistle the blow,

Of all I see and fail to know,

# Lola

So slow to see and fast to call,

Like it is I want it all,

And all my want is all unsightly,

Backsliding surely and longing tritely,

Seizures seize a silhouette of reason,

And now they have lost control.


For all was foretold

So rare and true—

Like the sky

So vast and blue.


In the house settle,

And adorn not the sun,

For surly the ground-stricken hands will fail

To beatify the glowing one!


Retract, reset, resilhouette, restore,

I am open, so give me more.

Ponder betwixt extravagant and bland,

To feel the power of the mighty hand,

So he calls and I cannot look away,

Upon the world, upon forever,

Upon the only love I know.

5

As if all the worlds unlatched,

Her beauty goes unmatched,

Attached to the void

From whence I sing her praise,

And such things it is each psalm portrays.


He slays the sweeter scent,

To wonder then just what it meant,

And so righteousness is always

Lost within the folds,

Like it is the devil's eyes he holds.


They wander without wonder,

And step together and step asunder.

They take us in their arms.

They leave us broken hearts.

And so together, they build our moving parts.


Parts of the sky or scents of the moon,

We come together so fast,

Only to form a departure so soon.

I cannot tweak the senses,

Nor ride the swaying grid,

But if it was done before,

Then surely it was I that did.


I the sun, I the moon, I the dying man,

I have left the orchard's womb

With death still on my hand.

6

It is forever now

Where chariots fly from wells of grounded thought,

And fires blaze upon devils' pinions.

Angels sore, meshed in color—

The moments are unbounded and free.

Swallowing with hue every mortal interstice,

The fabric grand and unchained

Follows one humbly.


From the sunlit sky hangs the celestial chandelier,

And through the forest green

Traverses the stream

Of the bubbly mere.

Sips the water the deer,

Alone this gentle doe,

Athwart goes the butterfly,

Swinging to and fro.


Splendid waves of green

Dance with the zephyr old,

Flowers growing dear

Welcome the sun so gold.

Melodies form a shape of graceful sound,

And caress the heavenly curtain that hangs

From infinite to this earthly ground.


Through the floor of the kingdom

Nature's creatures creep,

While at the bottom of the river,

Sleeping pebbles sleep.

Birds cloven in black dot the sky,

And the omnipotent atmosphere

Holds the ones passing by.

Warmth is not alone—

With the earth it shares its heat.

Living in my soul,

Its light is ever so sweet.


An immortal imagination leads to a place

Where neither words nor glances can penetrate the eye.

I saw the tender child, trembling,

Being strangled with a cry.

With my hand I brought him to his feet,

And together we walked

Down a moonlit street.


A reflection of our stroll

The ocean to hold,

Like an unforgiving prophecy

The sky once told.

"Why do you believe in a crestfallen heart,"

I asked with simple way.

Shrugged shoulders exhaled with shaken head,

The answer he could not say.

And then the ocean opened,

With a glint we were gone,

And then stood still the peaceful water,

Like forever us it had forgone.


A white place, like pinions of a dove,

So soft and serene,

The silence speaks of love.

There we stood enchanted and with awe.

Fragile steps moved not forward,

For in our eyes nothing we saw.

Again the child began to weep,

Declaring his sorrow his own to keep.

And I with gentle eye stood idly by

Listening to the psalm.

And then I let my fingers sooth his gentle palm.

"Oh why, oh why, have you brought me nowhere?

I was once content in the deepest despair.

But now I stand in empty white space,

Though true it be with heaven laced,

I see a vision of nothing ahead,

And morn the path my feet have tread."

His song so lovely clashed my soothing touch,

And all at once, the strings began as such:


A heavenly symphony of resurrecting joy,

Betwixt the snowy realm its notes deploy—

Timeless inspiration was its song.

Low I bent, and looked within the child's eye.

With one innocent kiss, I dried his cry.

"Now look again, and tell me what you see.

Is the land not grand, is the time not free?

And if so, whoever shall you be?"

The child saw, and was enveloped at once,

As above hung a celestial chandelier.

7

Help me see the light,

That I may step away

From terror and plight,

Through the night,

Tender and pale, where feelings

Belong to oceans bygone,

I may sleep.

And if it be

My childhood to weep,

And river mountains,

Their calm to creep,

Hillside steep, above to climb,

Death be murder this solemn crime—

And fear not away,

Like angels past

Looking through the looking-glass.


Till only you there was no more,

And then I left the stranger's door,

Walking around the twilight seemed,

And through the corpse the heavens gleamed,

Calling with fingers that rarely stood,

And I so brave I only could.

But you left me, and I was,

Still today looking through the fuzz,

Through starry eyes, though intentions old,

My burning body is burning cold.


Open flowers of tranquil air,

And look no-more the staring stare,

That looks unknown of living wombs,

And hides like shade in pilgrim tombs.

Lower then and still to go,

I ride the ocean—the endless flow—

That lifts me to another place—

A face no longer my own to bear.

Rare it was but never again,

Be my lover, my only friend.

Together we shall rise, together we shall fall,

And listen so free, to the tender call.

Raindrops of my heart

From living clouds fall,

The blinding light is all that I saw.


It is in your soul—

Your wayward soul—no other place.

The piths of joy are yours to chase,

Then hold them high, like the crystal glass,

Warming into time the sensual splash

That colors with iron the beating heart,

And holds together the ripping part

That once was fringed and ghastly tinged,

But only now subtly grows.

The ghost within curiously flows.

I follow so bravely wherever it goes—

A restless foot shows the way,

Like summer to follow the love of May.


Say there, O gentle one,

How will I know that truth's been done,

Or shall it be, destiny unknown,

My own sight is whence I've grown?

And if it be, atop the height of the highest tree,

Apples from orchards melting like gloom,

And witches riding the witch's broom,

Stones of the tomb running away,

The dead their own no more to stay,

Then in thorn-less roses may I peacefully lay,

As from dim-lit lanterns shadows openly say

All clandestine moments of yore—

No longer knocking on the knocking door.


Your love to me was never enough,

For I was strong, and brave, and tough,

But now I cry the worldly song,

With ceaseless enchanted nights.

With myriads mingling the tingling bell,

That in my head so randomly fell,

If only with reason, if only with grace,

I give all to you, this heavenly place.

A palace of knights, and moons in the sky,

The time was ours to let pass idly by,

Or take with passion the breathing air,

And say with meaning the every prayer,

And die like heroes so bravely earned,

And live tomorrow the truth you've learned.

## 8

The one that grows not old

In the cold no longer lives.

To black-heart lips he seemingly gives,

And makes mistakes a light to bear.

Endless candles within me burn,

As the fearless hands of time so turn,

Round, round, and round once more—

Cuckoo-clocks we do adore!

Wild wisdom wrongly came,

Though took my hand all the same,

And showed me to a place of sunshine feathers.

Weather this be yours, or this be mine,

The squirrels still run from sounds sublime.

Heed not this their crime, take not away,

For underneath the cracking bridge,

The children of love still play.


And when it comes this body still,

No longer a pulsing beat the arteries to feel,

Eyes that looked so much before,

Now to look a vacant store,

Hands that played every note,

Tied in silence the speechless throat,

Dead this body be, and decay—

Lay in grave below the ground,

For human life I gratefully found.


Think of me once, think of me then,

Tell me *I* was your only friend.

Lend me empathy, lend me a hand,

Up pick my grain from the common sand—

Just as I hoped, just as I planned,

Thus is the grain so grand.

9

I move like the wings of the cello's strings,

And rejoice in the sounds of a broken heart.

So priceless the pain, so benign the woe,

Through ardent eyes the life does show,

And showers upon us every grief,

And brings us still the falling leaf.

Winter, fall, spring, and summer,

Sleeping bears the winter slumber,

Number exponential the matting rabbits,

Refreshing joy of spring to come,

And now I've rhymed every one.

Milk, oats, and honey this meal,

A child robber, and love to steal.

Clasp my hands and squeeze so tight,

The night so vulnerable, yet filled with might,

Holds me just right, and never lets me fall,

Back and forth we throw the throwing ball.


Blow out the candles and make a wish.

Let catch the rod the swimming fish—

As dawn forewarns that he is near,

We tread the path with all our gear.

These are the days we never knew,

The grass so green, the sky so blue.

And you were there, and you are gone,

Long before I had a chance,

So now I speak of true romance.

Thus cries my stance, thus cries my sorrow—

Thus cries my plight of every morrow!


Do you love what I've become—

Do you love it all, or do you love it some?

Tongues of gold, and skies of red,

Down the white myself to sled—

One that led a life with mystical trace,

Distilling terror from his soft-grown face.


And in the wind my gentle call

Wakes the night and spirits all,

As you sleep, and now I cry,

For I saw you passing by:

In my head sings your song,

A countenance forgotten,

But your soul burns strong!


Burn strong the soul,

And melt me to pieces.

10

Creative brevity

Below sunken hills

That we climbed upon

With shattered bones,

Cast like stones in oceans grand,

Touched forever the believing sand.

Kismet held in god-skin hand

With flurry bushed in depth and worry

To journey the odyssey unknown,

And be the thrower of lightning thrown.

Shown to eyes of pulsing vein,

And scattered upon the time-bomb brain,

That ticks so lovingly of telling time,

And sings with sunsets the spoken mime.

The child to run through green valleys of fallen fables,

Tables upon set the delicate food.

Endeavors with chimes of endearing sound

Enduring feathers of metal-born weathers

To resist with gliding glee,

And in the tree of forever youth

Running feet no longer flee.


Be beside me—a table pure—

And drink with heart the curing cure

That quenches waterfalls with the driest sand.

Fanned upon blades of bleeding temper

Of vulnerable hugs alone to feel.


Crawling out of sewers of rats and poison fed.

Wed to a rainbow within every raindrop tear

Fallen from black that dries so clear:

Imperceptible skin and beating red heart.

## 11

The road to salvation lies just under your feet,

See the future from this fantasy street,

And follow so bravely you creator at heart,

For real love is passion, and passion is art.

So delicate, bold, special, and rare,

Whence the need to impart speaks so precious and fair,

Like scarlet spheres that glimmer in holiday trees,

And black that stripes the yellow bumblebees,

Grass to grow green and welcome the shade,

Swings that swung where the children played,

Dinners with families on new summer's eve,

The intricate webs the spiders do weave,

The tension of strings that vibrate the soul,

The music of Gods that renders us whole.


The perfectionist satisfied never at all,

Blind to the beauty of perfection we saw.

From manifestations of tragedies, unable to hide,

Like the smiling visages

that conceal this monster inside—

Indignant self-doubt to break thy breast

And fracture thy will,

Of realities created from what we did feel.

Thought to evolve complex and wise,

Lending to choice emotion's surmise,

Then wisely choosing with brow low,

And telling response just where to go!

Reclusive, despite volition,

Like the strong mountain ridge,

And then with intention to watch,

Keenly, every burning bridge.

The sundry selves sanguine indeed,

As to the higher intellect they reverently heed.

12

A symphony of ideas with tender motion

I have forged—I have declared.

And the moments in-between

Are perpendicular to the future,

And the future is parallel to the past.


Say what it's like;

Say not what it's not:


It's not brilliance at once,

It's not easy to be,

It's not heir of my dreams,

Nor absolutely free.


It's not pain in my hands,

It's not joy in my heart,

It's not understanding

That keeps us apart.


Not understanding is what draws us in two—

Living like poets so radically do!

It's like profound visions
In every sight,
It's like tired all day,
And sleepless all night,
It's like believing in one, so far from the sun,
And this "time" is my chance for redemption.

When before was the world so green?
It has become so
That the objects themselves are not what they seem.
When before did the red tree glow
As it stood like always it does?
What is forever if timeless it was?

What is the depth to which one can see?
I see more than ever, like glowing red tree.
How can the knowledge lie
Underneath what we already know?
However it is, it is certainly so.

13

Ballet; what is it to dance,

To touch the floor with delicate steps,

How is it to be?

To be a stranger in grace—

What shame, what sorrow—

Unless I myself become un-strange each morrow!


Fingers shall bend like never before,

Like feet that touch, so soft, the dancing floor.

Strings will learn to move the room, against all unease,

By which removes the sorrow,

By which forgets the thoughts that displease.

"Seize the day," our fathers taught,

And all to you, by them, was brought.


'Tis a journey like never before,

Though perhaps untrue,

As again and again I live once more!

But who am I to possess such a notion,

When countless days pass free of devotion?

Yet how can one long for life each day,

When buried deep within is one's timeless dismay?

However, yet again, perhaps untrue,

As death brings upon one a brand new hue!

But either way, I live today,

Regardless of emotion.

14

It rains where sense has no place—

It's deeper than wisdom.

Lilies of sunshine on broken land

That weep with desperate cries,

Taking us away, so fresh and free.

Fires of ashes burning with blazes

Of broken dreams, living cries

Of loving memories, to place the freedom.

Lips that lay lingering long

Over broken tenderness—

To helplessly hang from wooden frames

Of empty pictures

That steal from energy finite spaces.


But suddenly there was brisk light

By living mummies, holding their hands

That never will know

Of apples, and cinnamon, and carrots,

With laughing clowns' holly.

To brighten the school of orchards and farms,

That flew far from another world

Of holding your breath forever to come,

And always take it with simple tools

In wells of plight that bring no redemption.

Bending grass in the azure's blowing kiss

Of opening doors to white houses.

To step into a mirror and hold open the sun,

To then dive into the river and swim like the birds—

To beat with a black heart of sullen memories

That will not believe

That we lost hope, and we lost peace,

And who are we now?

15

I want to see the world through different eyes.

I want to fall victim to the visions of beautiful skies.

I want to think and feel

Of theories that seem so unreal,

Questions of science, matters of the soul,

Just trying to make my many I's a whole.


But what of this end's measure in worth?

Will this be my rebirth, my coming of age,

Or will it be nothing more than a passing stage?


Fall to nothing—these words—they may,

Though when it comes my time away has gone,

May they have led to a truth of self

I've hitherto forgone.

And that it be true in isolation I've grown,

I pray to find beauty

That will stand alone.

16

Whispers in the night,

Only levels of consciousness mask my spite,

Fairytales of something real,

So much more than we look or feel,

Stored in the library with books once read,

These fairytales become life within my head.

What's really real, who really knows,

Lose every moment,

And so it goes.

17

'Less I be caged like a show lion,

Shall I roam free.

Like a beam of light protrudes the dark of space,

May my presence be known.

My will is made from iron and steel.

My heart circulates the blood of a prince.

The spirit fights the flesh for livelihood,

And I bravely bear the suffering of this war.

I am a born again believer,

But what reality is I do not know.

I tremble in her arms as on I go.


I sit in peace,

Though I live in fear,

I contradict myself

As I cry no tear.

My empty tears fall unknown.

My fervent mind finds loneliness

In such an unimpassioned world.

The time it takes to count to ten

Leaves me more confused than ten seconds ago.

My manic brain

Lovingly shifts me to and fro.


I swear to my heart,

And I hope to die,

I sing when I'm sad,

And I laugh when I cry.

I long to change matter

With thought alone,

But I'm no Jesus,

Nor do I posses his throne.


So I accept my flesh,

And the bones of which it covers.

I accept the water,

Of which I cannot stand upon.

I accept the sky for all its heavenly color.

I accept waves as particles in the same.

I accept, humbly, my overwhelming fame.

I accept who I am not,

For only time separates who we are—
I am lonely in space, like inertia's law abiding star.


Philistine words falling from animals of prey,
Certainty of being proving the fools only way,
Fighting for identity in a pragmatic world,
Creating everlasting life after the darkest hours,
My eyes have grown weary
From seeing so much,
As arrogance speaks indifferently
From truth's unforgiving touch.


I refused to be swallowed by the mouth of the sea,
Only to be flooded with its peace.
A serene lighthouse on the distant shore
Meets colliding waves upon withered rocks.
The overcast clouds in the hidden blue sky
Rain the gloom of emotion on an otherwise perfect day.
And the green trees suggest a glow
Through this dark muck which too shall pass.

Every passing moment leaves us as empty as the last,

As the body desires pleasure

In this shallow physical world.

But my body desires my mind,

And my mind my soul—

I long to be one, I long to be whole.

18

Awaken my spirit and unravel my pain.

Mesh my fingers with strings of joy.

How may I count the days, lost in the absence of love?

For without, I fail to live. My spirit can be lost,

Deep inside the finite mass of this infinite mind.

But what is that which is called the body?

And why does it ache in pain—why must it live so stiff?

And the soul, how can a soul live free of its body?

It appears to be this ghost, working in harmony

With the corpse of my being, which merges into life.

So the soul and the body is my appearance.

But I shed a tear, and this tear falls to the ground,

And as it falls, I am stuck, I am still,

For every magnitude of its descent is captured

Within the depth of my eye.

The appearance of this soul, in this body,

Falls in this tear. And even this tear is alone.

A black road eagerly awaits the water of my heart.

How the darkness longs to murder me—

To steal the breath from my very lungs!

Why must it watch as free do I fall?

I grasp onto life, but she has not the strength

To hold my hand, though I forever love her so.


And as I fall, I look to the sky,

To that which they call heaven,

And as the heavens look upon my floundering body,

My mortal sorrow, the best I have to give,

It catches me not as it holds me so.

I fall. And within my fall I wait,

For all which is holy, and all which is good.

For if that which is good shall not swallow my evil,

Then that which is good shall not be my God!

If I long to live, however is it so

That my life has become a mere longing?

Though this longing, in all its misery,

On my weary shoulders

From whence its burden is carried,

This longing is the fruit of my labor.

For within my heart, my tender, passionate heart,

Within beats my longing, and my longing beats for love.

The world circulates through my oversensitive vessels,

Though my pulse cannot be heard, but how can this be?

How can the world, which lives within my soul,

Its anger and chaos, from tranquility and rest,

How can it not be heard? Or can it be so,

That the great journey, in its ethereal existence,

From years of laughing smiles,

And smiles that laugh in the face of pain,

Can it be that my ears have grown deaf? And if so,

Is the world not still beating within my heart?

For if the world beats I must live.


An atmosphere vibrates as sound escapes my lips—

Sound lost in space, and space curving with time.

But from where has this voice traveled?

Who is it that speaks? Must this be my soul?

But if my soul speaks,

Then who is it that captures its message?

Is there nothing more than that which I know? And why,

Why must there be, instead of being nothing at all?

It appears so, that if being were not in existence

Then no effect could be had. It's only in being

That nonbeing could be thought.


My words speak in circles,

Just as my mind longs to break feverish patterns,

And as matter lives within pi,

Like wheels role, and birds sing,

How rivers flow, and the tree is green,

How people laugh, and how people cry,

Mother, fathers, sons, and daughters,

Hopes, dreams, pain, regret, forgiveness,

And confusion—for this must be the circle of life.

But if life is a circle,

And a circle has not a beginning nor an end,

How can life? Or does it not?

For if it does, then what is before life,

And what before that, and before that?

And if it be an ending,

Then what after that, and after that, and after that?

How can one seek such truths?

For this very question must scare one beyond one's wit.

Does this fear not whisper within one's head?

And if it whispers, then what is it that whispers?

And if it whispers not, then what is it that whispers not?

Must I hide? Must I be a like a child,

And surrender to the security of my bed,

Deep below the covers that will keep safe my life?

Or must I stand, must I cry,

Shall I be naked in the rain, arms free, head back,

And as I stand, shall I scream

From the core of that which I fail to understand?

And will my cry hold strong against the lonely night?

By this lonely night, will my prayer be heard?

And if so, what next, and after that, and after that?

How far back must I look?


Through sight is life known. And life,

From the ear can it be heard.

But to hear I must listen, and only to look

Will I see. For the longing of my love

Desires to know life. But desire cannot be had,

'Less desire be an absolute.

For without absolute desire I do not live.

And what I live for is that sight and that sound.

Heaven holds my hand as she watches me walk,

But my hand is a hand of many, and so great a hand,

In accordance with the arm, and the arm the body,

And the body the soul, and the soul the sky,

And the sky the ground, and the ground the heavens,

And heaven hell—

So great a hand must it be.


The great honesty is beautiful in form,

From thus shall I live, and from thus must I speak.

For if I can speak the truth

For that which remains of my days,

Then how my days could be filled with love.

How I have hurried through days,

Just to meet a night that will soon end,

Which will then return to me the day—

What  a life to live, what a burden to hold.

So I shall hold open my hands,

and let fall a life once lived.

And as this past life hits the ground,

I shall watch as it breaks.

I will let my eye follow every piece.

And as I watch these broken pieces,

Which have fallen to the ground,

I will awaken my soul. And as my soul awakens,

So shall my body, for they are one,

Living in harmony,

Though within a chaotic world must it be.


A wonderful peace transcends

From the father above.

How these words were once told to me,

Once, when I was a child.

And those words did I believe.

But for some time a fallacy did they seem to be—

A lie spoken in truth,

And a truth from which all appears to be a lie.

And appearance, what must an appearance be

Other than what it looks?

And the looks of those words was all it was.

But that it was, and this it is.

So I sit and I stand,

all I come, all I go,

And from the depths of my being,

I have found my soul.

It was so that I, I, I…

I was one with the room,

From my body did I sit,

But from the body I was not.

19

The color of the sky is blue,

I trip and fall from an untied shoe,

The meeting between body and ground

Brings blood to my skin,

I bleed to death,

And my belongings are given to the next of kin.

All my value adds to nothing

In their hand,

For they see the glass,

But fail to see the sand.


Endless words spoken without sound,

Eight ounces becoming a pound,

My options were weighed with imaginary numbers,

Sweet dreams were found lost

Within endless slumbers.


My face grew thin,

And my hair grew long.

I was a saint in my eyes,

I could do no wrong.

I sat in my body,

Alabaster and still,

The seconds thrived,

Though time did kill.


The ladder between joy and sadness

I did perpetually step.

The tears of confusion were omniscient when wept.

The bewail of a man,

The struggle to stand,

The heart and the soul,

The half and the whole,

Lying smiles that would,

My perceptive sight that could

See the world for what it truly was,

See through the static,

See through the fuzz.


So the color of the sky is blue—

Things we forget,

Things we never really knew.

20

I tried counting sheep,

Though after a million

No longer could I go.

This linear line fails to bring rest—

I miss the lover,

The soft, the breast.


From the back of my head

My own two eyes have seen

The envy of those sitting still—

Lost in stare

About my wavy long hair.


Why must we sit in circles

And talk to walls?

Problems I create

When I see the future.

Solutions I do find

In creating truth—

Ah the joys of everlasting youth.

21

The living child

In a wondrous dance,

A spirit runs wild

In careless romance,

Faster and faster

Do they plea,

Spinning in circles

Must they be,

The living child

In a wondrous dance,

Laughs and smiles

In the spiritual trance.

22

May I scream to the God

That has stolen even his very meaning

From my heart?

This heart of mine,

Godless and cold,

Is growing weary,

Is growing old.

This heart of mine,

Under-loved and bitter,

Hates the same old words,

And is not a quitter.

This heart of mine,

Knows the sky,

Loves the stars,

Loves to cry.

23

Speak in dark alleys

Of ruthless love.

Run children,

Run through the valley of purple pumpkin trees.

Fall of edges,

And climb stairs to the bottom.

Trace circles with square hands,

And sleep well through the night.

Run children,

Run towards dusk.

Speak meaningless words

With the smartest of monkeys.

Swing through trees,

Like diamonds and pearls.

Cry tears of blood,

And drown in sin.

Run children,

Run for your lives.

Color outside the lines

With a mirror of vanity,

While standing above ant colonies

Pretending to be God.

Run children,

Run towards absolute zero.


How does one live!

Doleful tears fall from lonely eyes.

Heavy feet wallow in crestfallen melancholies.

Love is blood,

But what is the heart?

The answers lie within,

But what is within,

And what answers lie?

Endless skies to silence this vicious circle

Of linguistic complexity.

Water to rain in the souls of many.

Running children

Are growing weary.

Deep thought is only getting deeper.

Keep away the surface of the walking dead.

Trembling lips speak by the spinning head.

Muscles flex for the lens that captures,

For all is vanity in the end.

24

A winding road of misery

Through a majestic land of splendor,

To arise, fervently, from gloom,

Into the calm that love does render.

Winsome worlds of wonderful thought

At times to caress my mind.

In three dimensions I long to see,

But often in two am confined.

Breathe deeply the quiet air

Of the solemn night long,

Where only to be still

Would be to hear the celestial song

Of angels playing the sad melody sweet.

And learn to wait if deaf is the sound,

For all must fall from reason,

But true love can be found

In futures held with pensive hands.

So cease thy trembling and surrender thy woe,

Lest hands be unbelieving.

25

A pink-red sun

Bestowed upon the crowns of trees—

Trees bare with winter—

Branches missing leaves.


Awakening sun,

Give us your hand from the east.

Focus all attention

On the vision that you have seen.


The air is clean and cold,

And the old blue sky,

Birds gracefully fly in this ocean so blue,

All I see, all I do, comes to now,

The awe, the wow, the spirit inside,

Like the painter and brush, I abide by my sight.

Eye of my mind, eye of my soul,

Blood of my heart, passion of my will,

An excitement beyond the greatest thrill,

As that which is real has only fallen from imagination,

Endless hours of contemplation,

And the kid is on his way!


Such an elevated grandeur,

Where birds fly

In oceans of blue—

The pink-red sun awakens this city.

The pink-red sun awakens my dreams.

## 26

I continue to take steps to never before,

Like when you looked into my eyes

And said never once more.

Then I was gone and promised never to return,

Though forever I'll share with you the secrets I learn:

Thoughts deeper than three dimensions of space,

Greatly insecure eyes

Looking from the mirror to my face,

Emptiness filled with mathematical form,

As the soldier of your son lives on in the storm.

27

Amidst the void I seemed to be,

And the world appeared in flashing manic thoughts,

Spinning me around, that that world I was,

And my black glass body was an illusion of time,

When the world I was was twice sublime.

Then back to void the system fell.

Drank remnants my body from the illusion's well.

At once I fell, falling freely, from a rope that broke

With one pure stroke of genius tongue that was not mine.


When was it when we grew to see,

Or learned to stand for what we stood to be?

And how does the world become so small

When we fear to fly for we fear to fall?


Like projections, of three dimensions onto two,

This shadow that we call life falls from deeper too.

Thus I stand, budding like spring

From my bare bark bones,

Like a white-flower tree, giving all to you,

Lola

For you have given all to me.

28

God, the truly divine,

Have not you already walked the steps of my feet?

In navigating through the endless collection of words,

I have found great difficulty,

And at an age so young am at my wit's end!

The truth is only worshiped in silence—

An evanescent liberty unveils:

Within enlightenment is the prettiest time,

But what is this notion that sits forever?


The path is not faster, nor grows in complexity.

To walk with you is deeper just.

But I have fear of this solitude life,

And have yet to retain its abstruse trust.

Three states of matter, five senses to behold,

We fabricated your earth, and turned it to gold.

Three dimensions barely we understand,

And the forth pushes us along with its imaginary hand.

But to what destiny do we head,

And what freedom is the will that determinism led?

Seven continents divide atop this spherical place,

Inhabited by so many an insignificant face.

But oh to taste the fruit that grows from your tree,

And allow brilliant sunsets into the eyes that see!

29

Death whispers that I am real.

But in death, this reality is no more.

The truth lurks just around the corner,

And forever from it can we not hide.

The evolution of something wonderful—

We came from the trees.

We went to the moon!


Let us celebrate our feat,

Together as one,

For death is upon us,

And this race is soon to be done.

If not sooner, later,

But certainly will be.

The gods that live forever

Wave farewell to you and me.


The motion of mass-energy

We calculated so well.

We saw the celestial glue

That holds the world together,

Like gravity and the apple that fell.

We lived with love and pain,

With families, and in isolation,

Made meaning seem true,

Regardless of the honest situation,

Felt so greatly insecure,

But still walked with pride,

Built fences around our hearts,

Like pain that just couldn't hide.

We claimed to know it all,

And were ignorant in omniscience.

The way of the world is beautiful,

And beauty is insane.

30

Leave this body,

And step into the light.

Watch in awe

The bird in flight.

Half lit moons

In beautiful skies

Allow heaven

Into bewildered eyes.

The clouds are pink,

And purple too.

The wind spoke kindly

When it blew.

Blue skies gone away

To the coming night.

Rotation of Earth

Stealing the light.

Nature whispers

When she's near,

"Have peace,

I am love my dear."

## 31

Long ago and perhaps longer more,

There was a hill and a locking door

That myriads made an attempt to open before,

But closed it stayed with weather-worn wood.

The steep was green raised amid an open plain,

And a one lane road loamy paved

Saved the chance of an entering way,

And brought the summer children, oft, to play.


Bikes, balls, and weapons for robbers

Adorned the days of the once young toddlers.

Feeling each degree of tender warmth,

And air like holiday in the clay we breathe,

Perceive with eyes that know no more

Than green hill amidst a plain, and a locking door.


Summers came just like they went,

And lent to time their imaginary number,

That one wakes to find, unless 'tis left in slumber:

That all looks the same whenever unseen,

Though learns to look unlike the true light gleam!

Glint, gone, gathering near,

Guzzling down the earthly air,

Portals from reality asunder taking us there—

The unknown awaits surely to be found!


Summer sky blue kisses the beauteous day,

And on the hill, beside the door, a little one lay.

Play the children—play with heart—

And the stillness shouts from the moving part.

Three, three young ones there were:

One he, and two her.

One, as told before, laid beside the door,

The remaining two, with no avail,

In jolly and mirth, did freely sail.

'Twas like twenty-four hours of any other:

Each kissed their mother

As leaving for the mysterious day,

And when arrived at the place they oft did play

With all their hearts and sometimes more,

Not a thought one was given to the locking door.

For after so many summers past,

And sundry attempts to open,

Save a blowing blast,

At last the door became a myth

Of many stories told.


As the two ran like they were the storm,

And the hill held the other's bodily form,

The sun was yellow, the sky was poor blue,

And the breeze was quiet, as not it blew.

The one beside the door had fallen to sleep—

That of daydreaming, but hadn't gone to deep.

And then beside her stood a poet strange,

His eyes were squinting for the light had changed.

He was dressed in all black, and beautiful like time,

His beard was long, and his stance sublime.

He looked around at what was there,

And breathed deep the summer air.

At the sun-warm face of the daydreaming child,

The standing bard curiously smiled.

His silhouette eclipsed the sleeping one's face

Whose heart instantaneously did frantically race,

As she leaped to her feet, then saw the door—

The door that was open

That had never been opened before!


Four running feet followed not far behind,

Once the other two had seen the vision now defined.

Two catching their breath beside the daydreamer stood,

And open was the door of weather-worn wood.

The beautiful bard not knowing what to do,

Surrendered to the ground, and watched a bird that flew.


"Who are you, and whence did you come?"

Asked the boy with all his might.

"Have not your fright—I'm as frightened as you.

'Twas the open door I did step through.

From where I came,

I can hardly say, but a place like this

I once surely did play. Now who before

Has left that door?"

The bard mused on his own deep thought,

Till the children replied,

"Not a soul! Not a soul before has left that door!"

Pondering still the poet sat,

As with this newly-come mischief

The children longed to chat.


A tear, then, like an icicle on the sun,

Fell from the bard's eye.

"Why do you cry?" the daydreamer spoke,

But then like a storm the weeping broke.

"Soak in your tears?

Wither like a flower in perpetual night?

Why so melancholy when the sun so bright?

Plight in your hands you hold?

Or us three, that inquisitively beside you be, you scold?"

"It is not that. It's that I grow old.

And this beautiful place I can no longer hold.

Through that door a world grows stale,

And although I wish it so,

Forever here I cannot hail!

Here I do not belong—

Only now to the common throng."

Thus went the psalm of the children and bard.


But the door was opened,

And never shall change.

Through it the poet walked often,

And often seemed strange

Within to him that foreign place.

But the eyes of his youth,

Still, forever he chased.

## 32

The sun smiled,

Then returned my heart,

And I asked, curiously, why he tore it apart.

He laughed, sighed, and then looked away,

The answers, he told me, he could not say.


"Accept the heart for what it will be,

For I am the light that covers the sea,

Take your peace, and run along,

When the heart is broke,

The mind grows strong,

So live, and breathe,

And fly away,

No tomorrow,

Just today."

33

What of this will

That I feel to be free,

And when I close my eyes

What is it I see?

When I stand, and I fall,

And I stand once again,

Could it be true that it's all just pretend?


And if so,

Why do you write the words

That come from this pen,

And I into the cycle of confusion, you send.

Why do you hold me tight until I look away,

Then throw me to the ground like children play?

For what more could you want me to be,

When I long for life, and I long to be free?

## 34

Am I not worthy of this grace

Because of this time and this place?

And who shall I be, if not to be free?

For as one thinks so does one become—

I am the light and warmth of the sun!


My hand is still and moves with repose,

Revealing my freedom and choices I chose.

Gleams a marble of truth to which I wed,

In this beautiful space outside of my head,

Where the act of a child covers my rage,

For freedom is mine, and the world but a stage!

35

When beauty smiled,

Like red roses sprinkled with dew,

The light of her face whispered to me, a kiss.

With her blinking eyes my beating heart closed:


Clouds held the storm. Darkness held the day.

The soulful ghost of my corpse moved still—

Raindrops leaving rainbows on its alabaster motion.


And when my heart did open, it was her I saw.

How the seconds seemed to last a lifetime!

Oh to forever stand in the circle

That encompasses her beauty.

## 36

My beloved, come sit with me if you please,

We'll share our sorrows, and grow old like the trees.

Like flowers to my eye, your blue is the sky

To reflect gentle light as it passes by.

Oh, beautiful day, beautiful day—

How we waste this life away.


I found contradiction in my longing

To be a moral man, but this I do not understand,

For am I not just a shape of matter,

Like castles built from the sand?


My beloved, only you can make me pure,

I am evil without you, and of this I'm sure!

I am bitter, my heart cold,

My hand is lonely, without yours to hold.

One kiss from your lips, and I believe.

Give me everything I could not conceive.


I'm lost in my skin and alone in my head.

But even to shed a tear is in vain,

For where is the sense in falling rain,

When beyond the purpose of its cycle,

It falls without gain?


The face of others I can no longer see,

For I am ashamed of them,

As I am of me.

My beloved, wherever could you be?

When will I know your kiss?

When…

Will I know your kiss?

## 37

Miles and miles

Away from here,

I know you hear me my dear.

I'm sending a message through the waves.

Traveling faster than the speed of light,

I'm haunting you

Through your senseless sight.


Every time you wonder why

You can't just let it be,

It's because I'm making you think of me.

I'm evil in ways you never knew.

I'm fighting your will in all you do.

When you find another you so adore,

I'll turn him into an average bore—

This door of your mind you cannot close.

This door of your mind you'll always find.


Fall to your knees,

And beg for mercy.

Fall to your knees,

And say you're weak.

Confess weakness

As you cry in pain.

Shed tears

As you recognize your folly.


Recognition of folly,

Foolish ascent,

Up towards heaven,

Celestial queen,

Royalty of your heart,

Passion of this man,

Gods we are,

Is what you'll see.


See with your eyes,

And then close them tight.

Fall asleep with visions of me,

And when I wake you

From this lovely dream,

Tell me of the nightmare

From which you awoke.


Share with me the words

Of which were spoke,

You innocent doll,

So fragile and dear,

This mystical child would love to hear

How for some reason you always kept me near.


In your heart

I'll always live,

Freedom of your mind

I'll never give,

In the darkest alleys

Is where I walk,

Nostalgic voices

When I talk,

Speaking in whispers:

"Think of me,"

Your one true love

I'll always be.

## 38

There is nothing more than first love.

All else is second to it.

And with loss thereof,

Sweet soft misery keeps each lover by her side.


Ne'er can one hide—

The lover he, nor the lover she—

For first love is the only

One we give ourselves to.


By misery we wait,

As our hearts hope to beat again,

Finding always in the recesses of our minds

Each other more

Than we ought to for our peace.

### 39

Apart from the heart that beats within the chest,

There is this feeling, to which even death offers no rest,

Outside of words it lingers and weeps,

And endless shapes it kills as forever it keeps.

Though how can forever be,

And why move at all if all is nothing more than destiny?

Too heavy to hold, too deep to fathom,

But I just have to be near as if it were a comely madam.

Never I to see her face,

Though her line of destiny my feet do trace.

Lies of freedom forever she tells,

And I'm just the writer of words she spells.

I'm just the flesh so far from the core.


But I'm heavenly like the bird,

And its graceful soar.

I'm fearless like the lion,

And its dominant roar.

I aspire like the mountain,

And its highest peak.

I believe that only to find is only to seek.

At times I feel her crying,

Like gardens in midday.

The sun shines upon us,

As like children we play:


The holy ghost of nothing thought,

Tied in chains your flowers brought,

Crying and lost of nothing more,

Beaten and broken on the nothing floor,

Giving you everything, with nothing to give,

Spinning in circles if no meaning to live,

Thunder, lightning, and clouds full of rain,

Muscles, bones, and memories of shame,

Pain and emotion that feel oh so deep,

Outside of words I linger and weep—

Kill me today, but still forever I'll keep.

40

Blessed mathematics, you swallow my woe,

Into the numbers I fall, with peace you show

The silence of beauty, to move my heart

Into logic and trust, thy great art

By which I leave the earth,

I give my ardor to you, for all it's worth.

Blessed is your holiness, out of chaos you rain,

From the child of madness, the prince of order you train.

Into your truth I awoke,

So close to reality with no words to be spoke

Of, like two pairs of eyes first in love.

Passion you move and awaken me from folly,

Like to deaf ears bells of holly.

41

The necessary words can ne'er be said,

Like the unfathomable life that lives outside of the head.

A musical staff away vertically runs,

Like other worlds and other suns.

Understand, but for a moment, the abstract notion,

Like a mind apart from time and motion,

To see that life is grander still,

And remember now only to breathe.

42

The moral of the story is told by the mime,

Each living life the reproduction of time,

And then to forgotten places is where it goes,

Like soulless bodies buried in rows.

To hope for more is done in vain,

Thus is every attraction that aspires the main,

Heaven synthesized from fear and dust,

As reason is showered upon desire and lust.


Become a role in society, and a teller of lies,

Tie words into circles, and think to be wise.

Love one selflessly for all that they do,

While denying that your care is only for you.

Hate the words that cut to your heart,

Look into the reflection, and tear its image apart,

Put the pieces together to what you wish to see,

And now you are beautiful, lovely, and free.


Be taken back, and then taken away,

Confirm your feet to the path that leads astray,

Think twice, but dare not think more,

Lest you lose the security of the common bore.


Arrogance and conceit filled to the brim,

Stumbling upon truth just on a whim.

Young at heart, though growing in age,

The poetic tongue belongs not to a passing stage.


It only grows extravagant, tender, and bare,

Like life that was given but never seemed fair.

Always it seems to venture from the point at hand,

Like navigation through this arcane land.


I gave to you my little air as I was being choked,

Waited to be burned, desperately,

Like cigarettes un-smoked,

You tossed me to the ground with one regretful throw,

And now I will fall obediently, painfully, and slow.

43

December leaves dwindling down,

Secretly mirroring our deepest longings,

Crying out—the tender child—naked and afraid

Of the surrounding world.

Un-amused

With the moderate motion of the modern mayhem,

My malice lurks, and smirks at the other side.

Good is the side, in the taciturn voice it does abide,

But covertly, secretly, clandestine, it shouts,

"Take this hand and show it to love!"


Conceal no more my majestic sphere—

From heavenly places 'tis consumed,

And with heavenly fragrance 'tis perfumed.

Oh to believe in peace, everlasting,

Eternal in me!

44

Trees bare form an organic canopy of wonder,

Under which I walk from pride asunder.

The dreary day is desolate and cold,

As light life-giving not does it hold.

The sepulcher of folly is framed with the past,

From whence the poetic spirit love longs forever to last.


Evil visages my own to imitate,

Hate radiating, insecurity, and shallow pride,

Falling so short from the greater side.


Slightly slipping from where things are stale,

Beauty, like music, the power to hail.

Hands so gently holding the world,

Eloquence in grace—the dancer twirled,


And then circled the sun in a single year.

Clear was her body save her beating red heart,

An invisible azure the blood did dart

Through with fervor so free,

And she is the love whom we long to be.


Her voice is euphony to envelope every dissonant wave.

She speaks so tender, and to this voice I am a slave.

I follow to wherever she goes—

A place so dark, but her spirit glows

Magnificent light—a beacon to show the way

Beyond the meager facade the body does portray.

Ringing bells serenely glide

Amidst the air of ticking time,

Bringing to remembrance, eternal,

This solemn place divine.

45

The tender sun dips below the mountain ridge,

Tender to fall, tender to rise,

And defies, always, every cunning notion of chance,

Like the solipsistic bard,

Secluded, isolated, alone in stance.

The great fire to bestow upon the sky a flaming hue.

My soul, its light to shine through.


Teach me to dance in so many ways,

Alone with you always,

Here with you now.

Show me to know how when

A line's end I've reached,

That I may gracefully place it so.

For I am not of the people, nor the state,

As a good poet claims to be,

But I, like he, am a fraud writing for history!

The truth, however, that I've seen is great—

It is of myself and nothing more,

So who will love me now?

46

Her strings make rainbows

With the light—taking me to that better place.

Glistening through my beastly body,

And rekindling my gentle soul,

With her essence I've become entwined—

Her essence, to envelope the entire mysterious world.

So simple she stands,

Like brilliance unveiled

For me to see with neutral eyes.


There's no time to stand alone:

I watch her sleep, dreaming—

So gentle her moan.

So close to my heart

I hold her like flowers.

Oh that these feelings forever

Shall only be ours.

47

I wish to be imprisoned in her summer,

That I could not leave,

Waiting for the sun to fall,

And towered upon my flesh

Her ceaseless beauty.


Love lingers patiently

Within the mysterious folds

That can only unfold themselves.

Awake my sleeping  muse,

For here for you my soul to use!

And set to the wind it moves with ease.

48

She smiles I think when I close my eyes.

I turn around and face her stare.

I love the times when it's only us

Where love stepped upon the broken land.


When I came to the garden rose

She lost a whisper in her ear.

I set her down and let her sleep,

And in her dreams she was my fear.

Wake me then and still I sleep,

For her dreams are mine to keep.


Then I longed to hold her hand,

And to give her my strength that holds the world.

She thanks me as I cut her in two,

But my eyes have grown crazy now.

With my hands I form her soul.


And so it was in gleaming time

That we danced at night's great ball.

In our heads we were the world,

Though in the world we were only our heads.

We made pillows from ashes of endless time,

And found comfort in only this.

49

And then the turning points

Turned to spears,

Awakening all my sleeping fears,

Within this sphere of turning mirrors

I cannot look away,

And echoes back all the words I do not say.

So I close my eyes

And pretend to see.

Locked in chains

I declare I'm free.


And if it was the only way,

Like dark is night,

And light is day,

So we moved along,

Like mummies in song,

Tampering about our broken limbs.

Came in gusts these inspired hymns,

And sung to you from instinctual whims.

50

When we sail upon the ocean madness

We touch with bleeding hands

Their beating hearts.

You are me, and I am you,

And everything temporary

We see right through.

We laugh like men possessed,

Ruled by pride and ego great,

And lead ourselves to our chosen fate.

We long to hear the softer sound

That we know to be there,

For us a sound that mustn't sound so rare,

So hear we must,

With passion mad,

And we shall glorify our tears so sad,

And touch so soft

The dancing floor.

51

My love we've lost the lyrics

That once sang in our heart,

For with you and I together,

One heart was not apart.

And now, so many years away you've gone,

But I see you from afar—

Look back—my love—

For I am standing there.

And my heart, oh, my heart…

My heart only beats.

52

Go on my son

And continue to believe.

There in your memory

You shake with terror,

But the light will shine through

And show you the way.


When you were young

You were foolish then,

And now you are foolish still.

So hold for me the world

While I put you in place,

Then let your pride fall to the ground,

For there in pride is where you walk,

And all is finite of what you talk,


You are not the heavens

But only an image of,

And so you must choose hate,

Or you must choose love.

Hate is in your heart,

And heavy is it carried,

So loose hate in all your life,

Lest with you it shall be buried.


And know that it was you I carried

From forever long ago.

And Oh! the places you think you see—

Not ever have you saw,

For the length of my second

Is greater than your counting all.

## 53

And so, the poet spoke to his God, saying:

"Sing to me a song,

That I may then sing all my life.

Let it be filled with joy,

That I may sing through all my strife.

For what is the loneliest thing,

That I may be lonelier than,

For only have I a single friend!


And you are he—

But oh—the majesty and beauty

Within your arms—

I humble myself before you,

Lest you hold me not forever long,

So sing to me a song,

My lord,

That I may then sing

All my life."

54

Where we sit is our heart's complete companion,

Arrested in the milk of skyway green,

Only that we would un-hold the dungeon

Of the falling sky,

For only then we shall be alive.

It was alright with me

When I saw your skin,

But then your eyes became my heart.

Of the grass was the moment one,

You and I in the perfect sun,

Although the shade hid our faces,

As with you I longed to go to deeper places,

To be a friend with evil none,

And show you how my feet once did run.


My twilight fish,

You stand in the night,

So innocent to see.

You are by the stem by the root,

Between the dirt,

From whence becomes the tree.

Of me the bailey strong,

With guts inner rotted,

And now only worsens,

For I've become the fool besotted.

Benumb not the heart I give to you.

Confute the loneliness I assert to be true.

Believe in me now in everything I do,

And I shall breathe—I promise—only for you.


The convalescent eyes could not

Controvert your beauty,

But the timid hand held the fear,

And walked away.


Kismet, it seems, is naught

But the assignment of meaning.

And so, if again you come my way,

Then perhaps fate be true.

## 55

Greatly have I been humbled,

For great was my arrogance.

And still they ride and revenge all rapture,

With claws of iron the claws to capture,

Then the beating beats bold and brazen,

Sliding serene and soft and sure,

So sweet to twinkle

And solemn to stand,

Open to loneliness with each open hand.


Still deeper and deeper and deeper

To go, or meeker and meeker and meeker

To grow, and flow furiously,

Fervently, freely, and forth so,

For from whence it comes

Is where I shall go.


Tiny specks of the whole wide world—

Oh the dancer, the dancer twirled!

Crystal shoes walk a golden sky,

A sky that covers a sheet of glass,

Where through the glass is a hero fallen,

And with all of his might, the hero's calling,

And falling from fantasy is tenderness to tarry,

With wide red eyes a burden to carry,

With knees that ache but lives that form,

Like doleful eyes the soul to mourn.


The ground has held us to its call,

And we stand so sure, lest surely we fall.

Upon a triangle spins the daylight sun,

Steel blood paths upon a broken shore,

A sea of surrenders sinking

Into black-holes of remembrance,

A vicious heart with a smile its semblance,

Independence daunting on the neighbor's broken door,

So as we want less, let us only want more!

## 56

I pray to God to make me strong,

To help me see where I belong.

I pray to be humbled,

For I know I'm weak,

Yet still it's always my pride to speak.

My pride is great,

For I am so greatly insecure.

And aside from love,

I have not yet found the cure.

## 57

I have surrounded the infinite brain,

And indeed, the madman is insane!

Let the quilt be springtime fresh—

In your heart the thoughts to mesh.

Led by the will of the time-travel foot,

Covered with confusion as of the blackness of soot,

Put the eye to the only place,

And let the unwavering hand prudently trace,

For the panorama view is always the same,

And indeed, the madman is insane!

58

I have stood

And confronted the Gods.

I told them, with a spirit wild within,

That I was the strength

That awakens the day.

"Know," I demanded,

"That I am strong!"

"Know," I declared,

"My love is true."

And so the Gods,

They love me in all I do.

## 59

Bracing blades of brimming light

Leap, though lost, slash, rise, and roar,

As the eyes of heaven within me do soar.

And my eyes, both, alone, adore

The silence of the stillness that sets the sun.

Run to be near me,

My precious child,

For the glowing of my head

Is calm but wild.


Left me you did,

And my heart was a trap.

But now I see,

Enclosed by lesser walls

Far removed from the greater world,

That here is not the majestic glare,

Nor the whispers of beauty that speak so rare,

Nor the sparkles of time

That fade away,

Nor the sun, nor the moon,

Nor the night, nor the day.


The grey falls, like a triumph of will,

And the stickiness of torture

Does out easily spill,

Severing my doom

And chambers of pain,

Incident light of the glory so plain.

Run my child, and me do be near,

For he has given us life

And taken our fear.

He has paved the way for us to follow,

And filled our beating hearts so hollow.

## 60

So what is the one

That steps as the seed,

And so too is it the same

That speaks as the greed?

Plead, plead, oh plead gentle one,

Pulchritude of peasants placed as the sun,

That surrounds the landscape, and levels the sea,

Though always unsure of what it will be,

Beyond measure of breath and tongue,

Eyes of the old, heart of the young,

Yearning and longing and desperate and free,

Standing so simple like the stance of the tree,

Tied into roses that are tied into time,

Feelings of depression against feelings sublime,

Such is my crime when I am the innocent,

And such is my depth when I am the free,

Tarry and tally and tender hands rise,

Sees with resolution the tender one's eyes,

Lost in a world, lost in a dream,

Dreaming of walking the balancing beam,

But barely beholding the breadth below—

In fields of delusion the seed to sew.

So decipher the date and declare the meaning,

For all that it is is all that it's seeming

To be, to bane, to from greater things refrain,

Refracting like a prism light into parts.

## 61

I saw the stars from the past,

As though looking from the future.

And the night sky it was vast,

As though looking in a dream.

It was unbelievable in the heavens—

So simple, brisk, and clean.

62

My mother my father,

They live by my side,

Though long ago it was they died.

My sister my brother,

So we did lack,

But not would I take one second back.


How it is we wonder,

As we know no one will understand.

How it is we're full,

As onto emptiness holds each hand.


How it is we're deep,

Beyond any avaricious asperity.

And so in the softness of solitude,

It was we searched for clarity.

63

My heart becomes tender—

Greater than grave rages of despair.

My eyes stare and stare

At the beauty of beauty's bone,

Alone, calling from beyond my own name,

Equally same to the dying ground,

But separate, far, from my neighbor's love,

Or idea of, for only I know truth—

The mind be humbled,

The will be passion,

The eyes be youth.


I went where no one knew me,

And with their eyes they saw right through me.

And I discovered thought, like sweet vine

To elegantly entwine with a growing storm

To never rain,

And resonate, like madness, in my brain.


I have heard the names of many men,

And of them, not one I name my friend,

But I love, with sparkling eyes, this miracle,

And I feel every perfect cry

That cries to me with imperfection,

But cries to me with purpose.

### 64

We fear, but we are strong.

We love, but we are weak.

## 65

Oh that I could be the one

To alleviate your qualm,

And lift—lift you to another realm,

Where seabirds sing, and songfish fly,

Like fairytales or fantasy enveloped by the sky.

Oh that I could be the one

To hope inside you give,

For meager am I in truth,

And in my words I live.


Meditate upon my madness,

Muse upon my whim,

And know that my soul is light—

Just as it is grim.


Oh how I love you for your eyes

That tear upon the page,

And love you for your kindness

That speaks despite your rage.

So let us let the night

Dazzle the light-struck moon,

Forgiving the ancient wine

As it warms our deceiving blood.

Let us let the stars

Remind us of how far we've come,

To only tell us then

How far away we are!

66

Words so dark and vast and swift,

To lift and linger, sail and send,

Mending the frail night call,

Shouting the voice like a dancing ball,

And he was beaten, before, bewailed,

Brazen winds boats that sailed,

But now he cuts a buoyant air.


Slick and cunning sideways sweep,

A frigid fortune to finally reap,

Rapping like clouds and tapping like rain,

A brain bewildered billows ablaze.

A phase, a feast, a rigid noon sun,

A secrete serene and light-footed one.

Watch as all does fall to now,

Like what I saw I knew not how,

Nor why, nor when, nor we, nor they,

Nor summer, nor spring, nor night, nor day,

But lying around and lying about—

Transforming with belief such indolent doubt!

## 67

Grim in the deep dark cages

A sullen heart fiercely rages,

Ranting wildly and childishly seeking

The waywardness of forever fading away.

But no! not now—not this day—

Declares the doom-diddled dainty son,

Seeking sullen heart fiercely one,

Wondering wildly with wages unmatched,

Surrounded by madness but sweetly detached,

Sweet the world and all its place,

So light the steps with all their grace.


Gracious giving gathering here,

Near to heart the oak tree firm,

Foretold fantastically the fable-built stern,

Stuck in a sideways ceiling sweep,

From numbers to tongue the tales to creep,

And keep, and kindle, and spin like a spindle,

For they were spat and spread

And moved like the windle,

Winding down and turning up,

And filling over the hollow black cup!

## 68

Deep in the wind gust halls,

Halos on men and murder with dice,

A devil dances and declares the dungeon grim.

Grieve with smiles and saints of madness,

Sadness savory so sweet and sure

With pure pleasure bleeding the eyes.


Envelope the world with stars of light,

And marvel with wonder and marvel the sight.

Shoot the dashing arrow swift and stealth,

Robbing the time of all its wealth,

Because the eyes they see

And the ears they hear,

So we long only to hold the wind!


And the hands are wiry and fierce with passion,

Giving breath to the lungs that breathe,

And breathing so fresh the air—

And oh how we dare to daintily dance so soft and fair!

Forging riddles and ranting about,

Not to do without, love so grim,

Loosing ourselves just on a whim—

Barely holding on but above all the world,

Above its beauty, above its madness,

Above its mysterious mask,

And what is it all is all we can ask!


And ask and tell and the witch's one spell,

To spangle a series of green gallant songs,

Longs the heart, leaping and latent,

Gigantic and warm—a storm ascending

In the crates below.

69

Mother me Joseph javelin jubilant joy

Destroying the peace of her indolent boy,

Breathing breath brisk bright though bashful,

Where up above the rise has rung.


And screaming with joy

And melting with mercy,

Pelting with stones a delightful devil.

Revel all thee, revel all they,

Hiding in your baskets the greatness of day!

Developing with cunning a tree of youth—

Have not you heard it was all a spoof?

Spoof spoke he hidden in darkness.

Spoof spoke he hidden in light!


Now the rituals had raised their goblets of gander,

When he set his heart upon their feast.

A ghostly gloom gathered like dust,

As all began to question the ones they did trust.

Now rust fills their eyes and souls,

As blood-red wine leaves the silver bowls—

Silver from earth and spirits for mirth,

But the mouths are lost in a tireless tarry.


And he'd carry them out and let them behold,

But only then his loneliness they'd scold—

Old and young, tired and weary,

Lost in thought, depth, and query.

And now the rust rattles

Till it breaks free,

Then with agonizing voices

The agony does plea.

The earth is dark

And filled with pain,

And love has never seemed so bleak,

As for warm studded hearts it does valiantly seek.


Set upon a sunset of heavenly rays,

A rush of gold within, a timeless chant,

An openhearted fool to foolishly rant,

Radiation of madness and much all the same—

A beast within only to tame.


Lame footed mummies hoarding our heaven,

And of the deadly horses I only saw seven.

Surely it was something out of a dream—

Electricity, magnetism, or a timeless beam!

Beaming through space or time all alone,

Seeing so abstractly all that's been shown,

Now, before, even forever,

Like of all the cunning, the one most clever,

To severe our loss and into joy leap,

Or so it is such love to creep.

70

Wrap around the night fingers silk and swift,

And let lift from hands

All burdens in drowned and carried.

And the feet they've tarried and torched the hide,

Lingering in depths so deep and wide—

Wide eyed and whisper fair,

A sweet whispering amidst the air,

Oh how soft and sleek it rides,

When surely the walk forgets its course,

And of inspiration there is no source!


Between the eyes that fall upon me,

My own measurement delayed, or so betrayed,

Betrayed but so, so forth to go

Into a likeness far unlikely,

Far where shadows shear the storm,

A heavenly creature within a bodily form,

A form that rises then falls away,

But holds the night, and holds the day.

And what I say I say to you,

You of whom without I grew.

Grieves the heart in places unseen,

And bordered with gloom the eyes so keen,

Crafty and crazy, crooked and crutch,

And so on and so on, and such and such,

But I guess I'm just trying to say

I miss you so much.

71

Tears, pain, and love,

From up above godly eyes behold,

And as already it's been told, unfolds the story.

Temperature, tension, and ticking sideways clocks,

Defying gravity these floating onward rocks,

So it ticks and it tocks

And locks the eye on an unbound redemption.

Redeem, reset, and raise all voices,

Razor sharp and liquid thin—

Kin to the heart, and kin to the mercy.


Tours the seven deadly seasons,

As saints guide him in his sepulcher of service,

And with divine hands behind the reasons,

How could I forsake the past?

So with death summoning me to his barren ground,

These words for all that shall always last!


Last forever and illuminate the darkness,

For so low this head has hung,

And sung surely only to survive,

When insanity was never a choice nor a truth,

But the eyes looked harder as they looked aloof,

Atop the roof of a burning house

That burns love's kindness in its savage breath,

By the fern, by the folly,

By the laughing clowns' holly,

Jolly and jubilant and deadly and deceiving,

With a thread of destiny the weaving hands weaving,

And so the eyes—they were perceiving.

72

The fire ablaze will take him to his ashes.

Upon the pyre he burns and billows.

The willows that weep droop from the western sun,

Sounding the void with life and love.


Lay upon two eyes two golden coins,

Eyes once captive to interpretations crestfallen.

Forging into memory the unloved son

An unfolding of time sweet and serene.


Hangs on the hour every broken dream,

Seeming to awaken into life's pure touch.

Severe so bashful she cries with beauty,

But the beast of man betrays her bidding.


Murder lingers in the heart and soul,

When what we were was never still.

And freedom was a door to enter.

And beauty was only to call her name.

The sky now torched with tyrants of folly

Laughs out loud with all its joy,

For he that burns was not a man,

But he that burns was just a boy.


By then the fire flamed with black clouds of rage,

Burning fiercely above the burning stage,

And all around were empty spaces,

Filled not with loved ones crying faces.


A heartache for peace beat so boldly

Once below bones battered and bruised.

But where was peace but all around,

And how then could he not see?


Death, how it is you rose

Every morning like the rising sun,

When all you were was but a moment

Of endless moments to come and go.


Here burns he, a soul set free,

Wishing for love's grace.

Bereaves he now, pensive to stand,

To then silently leave his place.


Now where he goes is not his to say,

Nor solely out of his hands—

Hands blemished with inability of will,

Unless he sees that he is at fault.


For if he pray, he must truly believe,

And when he falls, let him fall all the way,

For in each instant so easily missed

Was inspiration enough to live in forever.

73

Come to me the silence

That stands in the wait.

Bring with you the patience

That steadies the gait.

There, somewhere, between

The method and the madness,

The only real discovery

Was the realization of true love.

Lola

# BOOK TWO

# Lola

74

Lips so deep as wells and oceans,

Swells the eye of every sight,

In the hardness of truth

And the disgrace of intention,

Where lingers all doubt in the halls of pretension.


Married to the buried skull

A wristwatch shadow or light so dull,

To drag me under dirt and leaves,

And stone and root and wretch,

To vainly throw and fetch,

And catch a tracing hand

Tracing a corpse's beating heart.


With two grins and a drum to rattle,

Ridden on the horse and saddle

Of daunting looks and descending stairs,

Withering with insecurity from envious glares,

Though by a shark-tooth spit and sticking glue,

Was made him fresh and made him new!

Nor end the spinning children,

Nor set them on their edge,

Nor hope that they were lost,

Languishing on their ledge,

Rather ripen the orchard key,

Letting it walk on stilts,

And cover it with warmth,

Like homemade warming quilts.


Doors to enter rooms

Where rooms where not once before,

And ceilings to stretch the skies—

An outstretch to stretch the more!


Mask me with a minute,

Bore me with an hour—

Burn in death the sweet;

Burn in death the sour.


Silk the deceiving mistress,

Ruby the radiant glow,

Bring me now so high,

And take me then so low.


Where I wait before you,

Where I wait instead:

The bear-claw sword

Stabbed through the pallid hide,

With a palace of saints

To in this wound abide.


So measure me with a dream,

And dream of what I measured,

Overcoming me like an artist,

Arranging the airy tone,

A white-letter alphabet,

A color sea in words,

An elevation of the mind,

And flying of the birds.


Wooden graves of laughter,

Laughing graves of air,

Ticking clocks of madness,

And madness the staring stare.

Endless skies of forgiveness,

Forgiving skies of grace,

A countenance thenceforth forgotten,

Though 'twas so lovely and bright a face.


Face me with a love

That will wickedness deface.

Trace me with the stars,

And all their solemn grace.

Place me in the ruins

Of a wretched man's inner dwelling,

And gild it like a lily,

And light it like the telling,

Of tenderness unharmed,

Of a time unmentioned,

Of a will unbroken,

And kindness one—

Tell us of this story,

Tell us of this son.

75

Romance, in the black swirl of torture,

Lifted by the feathers of youth,

And fastened to the furious pulse of pulchritude,

Arranged with sunshine, displayed with insecurity,

Alone, by the tender hand.


Hast not mine eyes thy will,

And thy will mine eyes,

Set to stars and song

To burn through night like fireflies?


Where the ocean meets the sky,

And the mountain meets the ground,

Where heaven in grasp becomes,

Here too am I found.


Lift me like a mother

That never let me fall.

Hold me like a father

That stood for me so tall.

Red-veined mine eyes adore thee,

So why must thou abhor me,

For if thy perfect cloak

For surely must I wait,

Then surely am I held

Within thy perfect hate!


Sate me with thy flesh

That unfolds the crooked maze,

And let them count my beauty

When it is they count my days.


When it is they count my days,

And tally the marrow harp,

So sharp the studded fragrance of life,

So insipid the moments in-between,

With a sigh my breath will whisper,

And with comfort my consternation gleam.


Freshness come this newborn child,

And wake the sleeping one absurd.

Speak to us with many voices,

And let this brilliant voice be heard.

76

This is where you must be!

Oh—oh do you see?

Perched atop the moon,

O'er plight and dreadful gloom,

O'er room of dreadful showers,

Passing sure' the hours

With mints and mist aloof,

A disbelievers only proof,

This cutting time and hanging head,

The lurking snake of coming dread,

To tread but trail so far behind,

As we explore this profound mind.


And thoughts to shine like truths untaken,

The mixture of vanity and depth before you shaken,

And set into a swirl and twirl of fancy findings,

The pages free of all their bindings,

Floating amidst the air

Every heartfelt word so rare,

So melodious their merry motion,

So mystical their endearing potion,

Harps upon the grass of blades,

And noontide suns, and evening shades,

And scents of summer, and sponges of sight,

Never to reach greatness, however, maybe it might,

And the night, so silent, so young, so free,

Perfect pass, and perfect be,

All around the endless dream,

A child my heart,

A dance my walk,

An ecstasy of living

And rambling my talk—

Take me to the poets' garden,

And let me linger there!


And the air is like cotton to hold—

Its balmy disposition the frigid to scold.

And I scale it with numbers,

And I name it with love.

And the trees are like tyrants

To rule me with joy.

And the grass so green more joy only brings,

On which I walk so light' as if walking on springs.

Then sings my soul, aloud, at last,

Un-fearful of judgment and all of its past.

Pleases the awareness the every thought.

Comes out from hiding the secrete places sought.

Sips for refreshment the simple standing throne,

For gone is the bewilderment and clamorous tone.

Endless the environs and standing space,

And of beauty, and beauty, and beauty a face!

77

I want my sayings to forever last,

And last forevermore,

For they were said in beauty:

Beauty within the mirror,

With eyes to see never so clear',

Here, my youth, it is upon me,

And never better shall I be!

Oh for you to see, as I do now,

To stand, to perform, to take a bow,

And fill their eyes with wonder—

A wonder it is, though it is they know not how.


And know always now that now it was

That all you are was born in mind,

For surely you are not—not of the other kind.

But surely you're the one to only be

Master of your own sweet destiny,

Deciding time only in your favor,

A love built strong built never to wavier,

Built upon the sea, built upon the sky,

And so it is we live, and so it is we die!


Death, I laugh before you, and leave you in your place,

For life's upon me now, and I within her grace.

See my face, traced with love's own hand,

Move not apace, as it surveys the beauteous land.

And conceal me not in form, O Shakespeare,

For  I am free and wild.

Let madness be still this voice,

For I am still his child.


Let inspiration be my song,

And sing such songs shall I.

Let me be perfect and do no wrong,

And so I'll tell a lie.

Conjured up in youth, in the blackness of night,

Clever words unmatched, endless stacks of might.

And true my words be fierce,

Murdering the weak-hearted sort,

But to me they were given,

Thus such words are not my tort.

Take them with you now, and wear upon your brow,

Bereaving not, and weaving so,

Never from you to let them go.

78

Alone, in the wild night's mansion,

Set to words each without a name,

Tempts the ghost, deluded with strangeness,

Yet the stranger I follow behind.


Drive apart the veins,

And set them down with fire.

A reaching out has led within.

What misery taunts me?

What ocean-less Earth unfolds?

Come apart these broken limbs.

Hold no more the one that holds!


What paints the sky with freshness

When eyes so rarely see?—

By case-less eyes I've held the sun

And warped about the timeless halls,

Where reason strangles the voice of love,

Alluding to a gem or ancient path of wisdom,

But deeper within I've felt their folly,

Where the halls become a source of great despair.

79

A purer touch, this gentle hand,

Cries a whisper tear.

What love! What labor!

A static plunge into this brazen sea—

This crooked way and beggar's fee.

From the noose of necessity hangs a soul to plead,

But most this need is want, and all this want is greed.


A stitched eye and swollen tongue,

Bruised and false and coarse,

Beaten by the swampy waters,

Driven by their force.

What holds one in one's silence?

What brings one to one's wait?

What weight between it is one carries—

A between that one can't sate!

80

Tweak the senses with other hearts,

And move so true the moving parts.


A twilight realm and starfish sea,

Upon me now, upon me free.

Fog this clouded night and day,

Where children sleep and children play.

Passed away the dungeon frost.

Lost in oceans the clouded sea.

Holding above the head the falling sky,

While keeping above its perilous charm to daftly try.


A hand of flesh and heart of gold,

A timeless story of time told,

A telling whisper wink and wage,

With soft red lips the speaking sage,

The page to cover with rare unveilings,

The stretch to sink into a squeeze,

Black-red blood by the half-born cage,

Bleeds inside within the half-born sage.

And all the cries are but a jest,

So move to dirt to become likewise lest!

Move to dirt the grasping of the ground.

Move to dirt the devilish sound.

And unwound the eyes become,

By a door beyond the self.

## 81

Escape the heavens and brimming massless sea,

Grim in their depth of anguish and simplicity,

Free in their overbearing, careless in their pride,

And walk with me here—here on the softer side.


Deep in these timeless halls a standing place is found,

And beauty calls and beauty sees,

Strong like the mountains and wise like the trees.

A tilted air teeters about a ticking moment.

A rise raises so rare from far below.

Thus I stand to be taken higher,

Yet this taking is only deeper to go.


Every passage falls to ruin,

Raped by the desire to create the past.

Short of the rabbit-hole hails the alphabetical song,

But hold that tune no more, lest you've held too long!

And I am a crush that never ended.

And I am a world broken un-mended.

And I am the hand a giving one lent.

And I am the savior a saving one sent.


But please pardon my daft coarse voice,

For I have discovered that each word is my choice,

And how can I be humble in all I say and do,

When in such things I long to be true?


And truth is a flower that grows in the dark—

She is like lightning, so marvelous to spark.

Every god and theorem she evades,

Though in her darkness, her brightness never fades.

She has been seen by many,

Dancing in the heart,

But she'll never come to power,

For that is not her part.


Oh how my eyes are fixed

On her elusive sway,

And how my tongue is eager

To reveal her like the day.

Like the day that stands in sunshine,

Like the night that brings us near,

She speaks every meaning,

And oh these words to hear!

## 82

The mass of heaven is lost without us.

Dead children are we within its grave.

Raised like orphans, planted in the heart of betrayal,

And abandoned to roam on the dusty ground,

Our sweetness is soaked with loss,

And leeks upon our tearful dreams,

So wake us from our sadness,

From where we were searching for home,

And on the dusty ground

Let us love to roam!


And how will we espy surrender?

And how will we serve like servants?

What frolicsome fields await

In the hands of coming fate

That will sate us with their perfection

And mend us with their ease?

Do with us as you please,

But please don't do us wrong,

For the target is our flesh,

And the bullet is our bone,

And when we look afar,

We're looking all alone.


But when we look alone

So far away we see,

And when we look long enough

We find the winding key.


And the world is a gear

That turns with the clouds,

And the law of man is a distraction

That true beauty shrouds,

And beauty is an ocean

That rages within,

Calling so solemn,

But still with a grin,

Greeting with grievance

And a purpose divine,

To send us with chills

That crawl up the spine.

So we crawl like infants,

And stand like warlords,

Naming with prayer

Your mercy and love.

We pray with blindness,

And believe with fastness,

And forge with fortitude

Our greatest hopes.


Has the world been without us,

Or only within?

Free are we now of all of our sin.

So shake us with sunshine,

And with riddles us feed,

For only to a truer heaven

Does every path lead.

83

These trembling walls speak of a ruthless will.

Arrangements of space become fairytales and delusions.

O my solitude! O my refuge!

Here, like a mad scientist, I have built myself.


My vision vast, and almost shapeless,

My tongue tied, though never weary,

In this place far, fast, and free,

Like hugs of insanity that long to be loved,

I have learned to walk,

I have learned to run,

I have learned to dance,

So let me learn to fly!


In my solitude I found my soul,

And in my soul I found eternity, and all there is to find.

And from eternity vanishes my soul,

But so too into it is it born,

Thus celebrate my death, but too it mourn.

And in the morning the sun shall rise,

And comfort with laughter, and comfort with cries.

In the morning the night shall fall,

And with wisdom whisper, and with winsomeness call.


I'll stand in two forevers

For a moment forever long,

And wash my eyes with water,

And sing my heart with song.


Oh these foolish moments,

Beyond any price,

Beyond any breath,

Wondrous like melody,

Harmony, rhythm, and clef.


Oh these countless hours,

Counted with a heavy heart,

Counted with trepidation,

Counted with thought,

Into gentleness and kindness,

And understanding brought.


And in this world I live,

And in this world I die,

But that I was unbound

Until I passed on by!


And this it is to fly,

Deeper than any fall,

Walking with pride for health—

Chest out, chin up, and tall!


And that I may learn to fly,

Leaving my solitude and chasing the sun,

Among men let me learn to recall

How to dance, walk, and run.

84

How obscure our passions!

How meager our delights!

Upon the moment waits my breath,

Unskillfully urging to utter my heart,

For there was once a time

When this rush of madness reached my soul—

A place like the common place around,

But subtly more vivid and truer more sound—

But now it is that I must wait, and learn to wait,

Ever so slightly, and a time far from long,

To catch my breath and utter not

Meager passions of pure delight,

But to journey—deeper—into the depths of my soul.


So cunningly I've manipulated words and rhyme,

Throwing chaos into order, and rhythm and time,

But from once those wounds and now these scares I see

That such nervous apparel was but a ghost to wear

In the freezing rain of my erupted woe,

Where the night became my eyes, and the world my hat,

That I could not stand to bear, for so heavily it sat.

Thus you heard it in my voice, and witnessed in my fall,

That of nothing I spoke, as with rapture I did call.


So let me call and walk the street,

And burn with understanding the fat of indolence!

Remove my hat and bathe me in the sun,

Removing from me my transparent form!

I walk the streets that from I vanish.

I build a house to abandon its treasure.

I fall to pieces from a touch so obsolete,

Holding tightly to a picture painted with folly.


My memory becomes a source of negligence,

Neglecting to remember such simple truths.

My pride is a prison, where in languishes my ease,

Leading me to pursue more complex forms.

Perhaps God is around me.

Perhaps God is within.

But I have not yet understood him,

nor known him truly.

So you, O God, is what I seek.

But I have been ashamed to utter your name,

And this shame is a shame of many.

Though perhaps 'tis not shame,

But rather doubt and shame,

And shame of doubt,

For I cannot know what you are!


Though like the light of a star,

Let me move a great distance from where I began.

Let me travel with speeds

In which they say passes no time,

Moving towards prose of deeper thought—

Only to embellish with rhyme.


Where can I find the strength to be honest in words,

When surely my words will only prove my ignorance?

How can I be enlightened, and move into knowledge,

When cowardly my words lack sufficient strength?

For my words have been a ladder,

And I have been in a hole of confusion

Trying to climb out.

## 85

At last it is to know,

On the wings of sacred youth,

That endless are the doctrines,

And endlessly insane,

For poesy be the only truth!

Sun sweet shine sun,

And shine sweet sun shine,

Grow the flowers that grow the time,

Like arrangements of disorder 'ever changing,

Where from here to there the range is ranging,

Like peace the soothing release from grief,

And grief the longing longed for most of all,

Like smiles are only hidden sadness

That reach so deep as to elevate the soul.

So all these lines were just a spoof,

Like poesy was the only truth!

Lola

Lola

Lola

Lola

www.ingramcontent.com/pod-product-compliance
Lightning Source LLC
Chambersburg PA
CBHW020954030426
42339CB00005B/99